The Search 1

Quotes by Albert Camus & Viktor Frankl

Therapeutic Journal Project #2

Compiled by

The FIG Project

The most thought-provoking thing in our thought-provoking time is that we are still not thinking. Martin Heidegger

Path of Self-Discovery

Viktor Frankl, a psychiatrist of world renown, wrote the book *Man's Search for Meaning* after being held a prisoner in a death camp during World War II. This is an absolutely fascinating and inspiring book about a man who realized that that he could go through any *what* if he had a *why* attached to it.

From his experience, both personally, in the concentration camp, as well as professionally, as a psychiatrist, he developed a school of therapeutic thought known as *logotherapy*. If you can attach a meaning to your experiences, and if you can find a purpose in your life, you will find satisfaction and fulfilment.

You and I aren't in a concentration camp situation, thankfully. However, we still have our struggles. And we still have a need to find meaning in our lives. One of the amazing ways that we can do this is through *introspection*, or looking inside to make sense and meaning out of our experiences. And a fabulous way to look inside is to get outside, onto paper (or electronically) what is happening internally.

One of the best means for this - a journal.

What works as good as counseling?

There was a study commissioned some time ago, by the counseling profession, to ask the question *Is there anything that works as good as counseling in helping people*? The focus was primarily on the issues of depression and anxiety.

The outcome was definitive. And summarily swept under the carpet!

Yes indeed -- it was discovered that there were two things that, if people participated in, would be as helpful to them as counseling. Two activities that worked as well as counseling, and that would give the same result as spending time (and money) in counseling. Two things that were, for all intents and purposes, free of charge, and fun to boot.

They were (wait for it...)

Gardening

Journal writing

That's right! People who either gardened, or wrote in a journal were found to be as benefitted by these as were those people who went to counseling!

Disclaimer

If you need a counselor, go see one. I say this not only as a release of liability for myself, but also because there are times that a counselor is necessary. Good friends are helpful, and I recommend them! But, some people simply need to be engaged in a therapeutic relationship with a counselor. For safety concerns.

So, in making the above statement about journals and gardening, I am NOT recommending that a person stop counseling, or not go to a counselor, when necessary. Please, if in doubt, see a counselor. Get help. Engage a partner with you on your journey through life. A counselor may be just that person.

What is a therapeutic journal?

You have probably used the terms diary and journal interchangably. But, there is a difference. Whereas a diary can be used to record the daily events and happenings of a person, a journal is more introspective in nature. A diary could, for most intents and purposes, be written by someone following you around during the day, recording where you went, who you spoke with, what you did and said. It's a recounting of the facts.

A journal, on the other hand, gets at what's inside you. How did you *feel* about who you spoke with? What was the *meaning* behind the experience you had earlier in the day? A journal tells the *deeper story*. It tells about your *experience*, which is more than just the observable facts.

So, a *therapeutic journal* is one that not only recounts the observable events, but also the unobservable thoughts and feelings about these events, *with the intent of you learning from them and being more* intentional *in using this to live your life on* purpose.

So often we *react* to life rather than *act*. The therapeutic journal is a tool that can be used to help you take charge. And by doing this, your freedom will increase. Freedom from going from once crisis to another, from living from paycheck to paycheck. Freedom from stress, worry, depression.

In journal writing, the internal and external experiences, thoughts, and feelings are captured. But with the therapeutic journal, these are not only captured, but then an intentional and purposeful direction is decided upon by you, and executed.

It is not an uncommon occurance for a person writing in a TJ to have a dialogue with herself. The purpose of this dialogue is to choose a new direction, through analyzing the red flags, issues, and concerns. The intentional life will come about. Meaning, that you will learn to live with intent. You create it, rather than have it create you.

How the TJ (Therapeutic Jounral) works

By recognizing and sorting out both your external and internal experiences, you will come to an increased *awareness* of what is happening. This awareness will lead to greater *insight*. Together, these will promote a *growth change* in you.

By writing in a TJ, you have a chance to *slow down*, something that is badly needed in today's world. Part of the problem in our current culture is that we are often *swept along* in life. We think and convince ourselves that our freedoms are bound and limited not by us so much as by what is available to us. And until we break free from this limiting attitude, which place we are in primarily because we don't slow down enough to realize that we really can be in charge of our own life, we'll keep going along where others want us to be.

A TJ offers the chance to bring clarity to issues that

otherwise hang out in the back of our mind, fuzzy. This lack of clarity has three major effects on us. First, it gives us the feeling that there is something incomplete. Something that we just can't 'put our finger on.'

Second, the lack of clarity and this feeling of being 'incomplete' create a stress, or anxiety, that is seems to constantly erode our peace of mind. It's like walking around with a ball and chain, feeling that there's something 'out there' to be done, but not knowing what is to be done, or even how to identify the problem. Kind of like being in a battle blindfolded.

And third, the lack of clarity disempowers us from making changes, because we can't change that which we can't see clearly. We feel discouraged, and so we simply give up. We allow defeat to come on us, before we even begin the battle.

What has the TJ been used for?

I believe that the biggest help that the TJ has to offer is to maximize life. Rather than just 'coast,' the TJ has the potential to help a person break free from mediocrity. Most people are just alive, without really living. Born - 1991; Died - 2019; Buried 2071. 52 years of expanding lungs, a beating heart, but no 'umphh,' no spirit.

There is nothing with which every man is so afraid as getting to know how enormously much he is capable of doing and becoming. -- Soren Kierkegaard

In addition to going forward from the middle, a TJ also has the potential to boost people up who still have to 'catch up.' to the masses. By this I mean if you struggle with depression, anxiety, trauma, loss, OCD, substance abuse, eating disorders, relationships, and self-worth, you may find this helpful. These are often co-occurring with other disorders, and are multi-faceted in how they exhibit themselves.

How to Journal

For some, writing isn't their forte. And that's OK. Because this is only one way to use this journal. It is a powerful way, to be sure. But in addition to writing, folks have found success by using:

Writing letters	Photographs
Writing a fictional dialogue	Making Lists
Writing longer fictional entries	Drawings

Timed entries - limiting the time you spend writing

Limitations

For individuals who have a cognitive processing or retention issue, TJ may not be that effective. The ability to think and process those thoughts is required. With practice, this can get better, of course. But at the same time, when processing is mostly absent to begin with, due to some genetic reason, or an accident, or drug use, a TJ will be of limited value.

Also, the ability to read and write is important. After all, even if words are NOT the primary conveyor of thoughts, they will still be utilized.

Lastly, if you've experienced a very traumatic situation, working through a counselor, face to face, should be considered. If you're simply the 'walking wounded,' you can probably handle this with the support of family or friends. But if you're a 'walking casulty' (no disrespect meant), you may need a professional to walk this journey with you.

Your well-being is the number one priority!

What will you find in this journal that is more than just blank pages?

Ninety pages, with a quote on each page. Feel free to address this in your entry.

Self-Knowledge pages

Vision page

Three *Letter-to-Myself* pages:

Past - Forgive; move on

Present - Convictions you've made

Future - Where you're going

Two *Letters-to-Others* pages: This journey is a 'we,' and you will impact others just as you are impacted by them. Tell them about it here.

Vision page

Genogram page. A visual diagram of your family and friend relationships.

Some Final Pointers

No person is an island. Some are more 'lone' than others, but all of us are who we are in relation to others. This is a 'we' journey and not just an 'I' journey. Keep in mind that your purpose in life, and your daily missions, will include others. When you set your vision, don't leave others out of it.

Write freely. Draw freely. Think freely. Break free from the crazy prison that you've been put in by society and expectations.

Be guided morally. So many people use their freedoms to make themselves slaves. To conventional thought, to substances, to limitations set by others. The moral way is the free way.

Keep what you write confidential. Because you do this, you will be more free to express yourself honestly. And honesty is vital to this process.

Though the quote that begins this journal, by Martin Heideger, talks of thinking, this is only part of this journey. The other part is *feeling*. The thinking has to do with the brain; the feeling has to do with the heart. Both are equally as important.

Lastly, return occasionally to what you've written. You will find yourself encouraged by some of the 'right' things you've written, and smile at some of the things you've written. You will find that some of your interpretations and conclusions are wrong. That's OK. Adapt and change. That's what makes you human.

Albert Camus:

Albert is a French philosopher, author and journalist, widely known for promoting the concept of "absurdism" -- the human conflict between seeking value and meaning in life and our inability to actually find them. He was born in poverty, and whilst still a youngester his family moved into a two room apartment. His mother, brother, grandmother, and a paralyzed uncle lived here. His mother was the primary breadwinner, working as a house-keeper to support her family.

In the later stages of his childhood, Albert had a desire to go into sports, and was inclined this direction in addition to being an excellent student. However, at age 17, he contracted tuberculosis, and his sports ambitions were put to a halt. He also desired to be an educator, but the disease also put a stop to that as well.

Still later in life, he received a Nobel Prize for Literature.

Viktor Frankl

Born in 1905 in Austria, Viktor Frankl is known as the founder of Logotherapy, one of the major philosophical thoughts in modern psychology. He was born into a Jewish heritage, and studied medicine at the University of Vienna, specializing in neurology and psychiatry. Early on he met and was influenced by Sigmund Freud and Alfred Adler, though he would diverge from their philosophies with his own.

In 1942, he was deported, along with his wife and parents, to occupied Czechoslovakia. He had the opportunity to go to the United States, but chose to not do this, primarily due to his allegiance to his belief that he had to remain with his parents to assist them. The result of this was that he was eventually transported to Auschwitz, and remained in custody of the Germans until he was liberated in 1945. His parents and wife were killed. A sister was the only other one in his family still alive, in Australia.

He went on to become a world-renowned psychiatrist and advocate of existential philosophies.

Thoughts

Thoughts

When you have once seen the glow of happiness on the face of a beloved person, you know that a man can have no vocation but to awaken that light on the faces surrounding him. Albert Camus

Always go too far, because that's where you'll find the truth.
Albert Camus

No matter how hard the world pushes against me, within me, there's something stronger – something better, pushing right back. Albert Camus

People hasten to judge in order not to be judged themselves.
Albert Camus

Life can be magnificent and overwhelming – that is the whole tragedy. Without beauty, love, or danger it would almost be easy to live. Albert Camus

You will never be happy if you continue to search for what happiness consists of. You will never live if you are looking for the meaning of life. Albert Camus

When the soul suffers too much, it develops a taste for misfortune. Albert Camus

Insight Question: Write a list of questions to which you urgently need answers.

Real generosity towards the future lies in giving all to the present.
Albert Camus

The only way to deal with an unfree world is to become so absolutely free that your very existence is an act of rebellion.
Albert Camus

It is the job of thinking people not to be on the side of the executioners. Albert Camus

To be happy, we must not be too concerned with others. Albert
Camus

In the depth of winter, I finally learned that within me there lay an invincible summer. Albert Camus

Man is the only creature who refuses to be what he is. Albert Camus

We all carry within us places of exile, our crimes, our ravages. Our task is not to unleash them on the world; it is to transform them in ourselves and others. Albert Camus

Seeking what is true is not seeking what is desirable. Albert Camus

The evil that is in the world almost always comes from ignorance, and good intentions may do as much harm as malevolence if they lack understanding. Albert Camus

Insight Question: What worries me most about the future?

Blessed are the hearts that can bend; they shall never be broken.
Albert Camus

Nobody realizes that some people expend tremendous energy merely to be normal. Albert Camus

I know that man is capable of great deeds. But if he isn't capable of great emotion, well, he leaves me cold. Albert Camus

There is no sun without shadow, and it is essential to know the night. Albert Camus

The need to be right – the sign of a vulgar mind. Albert Camus

Men must live and create. Live to the point of tears. Albert Camus

Life is the sum of all your choices. Albert Camus

I rebel; therefore I exist. Albert Camus

The struggle itself towards the heights is enough to fill a man's heart. One must imagine Sisyphus happy. Albert Camus.

Insight Question: If I weren't scared, what would I do?

Autumn is a second spring when every leaf is a flower. Albert Camus

You will never be happy if you continue to search for what happiness consists of. You will never live if you are looking for the meaning of life. Albert Camus

Don't walk behind me; I may not lead. Don't walk in front of me; I may not follow. Just walk beside me and be my friend. Albert Camus

Nobody realizes that some people expend tremendous energy merely to be normal. Albert Camus

Live to the point of tears. Albert Camus

You know what charm is: a way of getting the answer yes without having asked any clear question. Albert Camus

But in the end one needs more courage to live than to kill himself.
Albert Camus

When I look at my life and its secret colours, I feel like bursting into tears. Albert Camus

I may not have been sure about what really did interest me, but I was absolutely sure about what didn't. Albert Camus

Insight Question: What / Who did I make better today?

Real generosity towards the future lies in giving all to the present.
Albert Camus

An intellectual? Yes. And never deny it. An intellectual is someone whose mind watches itself. I like this, because I am happy to be both halves, the watcher and the watched. "Can they be brought together?" This is a practical question. We must get down to it. "I despise intelligence" really means: "I cannot bear my doubts." Albert Camus

Fiction is the lie through which we tell the truth. Albert Camus

To be happy, we must not be too concerned with others. Albert Camus

I opened myself to the gentle indifference of the world. Albert
Camus

The purpose of a writer is to keep civilization from destroying itself. Albert Camus

I used to advertise my loyalty and I don't believe there is a single person I loved that I didn't eventually betray. Albert Camus

In order to understand the world, one has to turn away from it on occasion. Albert Camus

At the heart of all beauty lies something inhuman. Albert
Camus

Insight Question: What do I want my life to be like in five years?

When the soul suffers too much, it develops a taste for misfortune. Albert Camus

Do not wait for the last judgment. It comes every day. Albert
Camus

People hasten to judge in order not to be judged themselves.
Albert Camus

I have no idea what's awaiting me, or what will happen when this all ends. For the moment I know this: there are sick people and they need curing. Albert Camus

There is not love of life without despair about life. Albert Camus

Man is always prey to his truths. Once he has admitted them, he cannot free himself from them. Albert Camus

I would rather live my life as if there is a god and die to find out there isn't, than live my life as if there isn't and die to find out there is. Albert Camus

Since we're all going to die, it's obvious that when and how don't matter. Albert Camus

Insight Question: Who are five people I really admire and whom I personally know? Ask one of them to be my mentor.

Some people talk in their sleep. Lecturers talk while other people sleep. Albert Camus

When you have once seen the glow of happiness on the face of a beloved person, you know that a man can have no vocation but to awaken that light on the faces surrounding him. Albert Camus

If something is going to happen to me, I want to be there. Albert Camus

Every act of rebellion expresses a nostalgia for innocence and an appeal to the essence of being. Albert Camus

It is the job of thinking people not to be on the side of the executioners. Albert Camus

There is scarcely any passion without struggle.

Victor Frankl

When we are no longer able to change a situation - we are challenged to change ourselves. Viktor E. Frankl

Between stimulus and response there is a space. In that space is our power to choose our response. In our response lies our growth and our freedom.   Viktor E. Frankl

Everything can be taken from a man but one thing: the last of human freedoms - to choose one's attitude in any given set of circumstances, to choose one's own way. Viktor E. Frankl

Everyone has his own specific vocation or mission in life; everyone must carry out a concrete assignment that demands fulfillment. Therein he cannot be replaced, nor can his life be repeated, thus, everyone's task is unique as his specific opportunity to implement it. Viktor E. Frankl

Insight Question: What is my 'why'?

Since Auschwitz, we know what man is capable of. And since Hiroshima, we know what is at stake. Viktor E. Frankl

For the meaning of life differs from man to man, from day to day and from hour to hour. What matters, therefore, is not the meaning of life in general but rather the specific meaning of a person's life at a given moment. Viktor E. Frankl

Challenging the meaning of life is the truest expression of the state of being human. Viktor E. Frankl

If there is a meaning in life at all, then there must be a meaning in suffering. Suffering is an ineradicable part of life, even as fate and death. Without suffering and death, human life cannot be complete. Viktor E. Frankl

Man is that being who invented the gas chambers of Auschwitz; however, he is also that being who entered those chambers upright, with the Lord's Prayer or the Shema Yisrael on his lips.
Viktor E. Frankl

In a position of utter desolation, when man cannot express himself in positive action, when his only achievement may consist in enduring his sufferings in the right way - an honorable way - in such a position man can, through loving contemplation of the image he carries of his beloved, achieve fulfillment.
Viktor E. Frankl

There is nothing in the world, I venture to say, that would so effectively help one to survive even the worst conditions as the knowledge that there is a meaning in one's life. Viktor E. Frankl

Insight Question: What should I be doing more of in my life?

A man who becomes conscious of the responsibility he bears toward a human being who affectionately waits for him, or to an unfinished work, will never be able to throw away his life. He knows the 'why' for his existence, and will be able to bear almost any 'how.' Viktor E. Frankl

A thought transfixed me: for the first time in my life, I saw the truth as it is set into song by so many poets, proclaimed as the final wisdom by so many thinkers. The truth - that love is the ultimate and the highest goal to which man can aspire. Viktor E. Frankl

Life can be pulled by goals just as surely as it can be pushed by drives. Viktor E. Frankl

Being human always points, and is directed, to something or someone, other than oneself - be it a meaning to fulfill or another human being to encounter. Viktor E. Frankl

Live as if you were living a second time, and as though you had acted wrongly the first time.   Viktor E. Frankl

Happiness must happen, and the same holds for success: you have to let it happen by not caring about it. Viktor E. Frankl

Ever more people today have the means to live, but no meaning to live for. Viktor E. Frankl

When I was taken to the concentration camp of Auschwitz, a manuscript of mine ready for publication was confiscated. Certainly, my deep desire to write this manuscript anew helped me to survive the rigors of the camps I was in. Viktor E. Frankl

Insight Question: What do I need to change about myself?

I recommend that the Statue of Liberty be supplemented by a Statue of Responsibility on the west coast.   Viktor E. Frankl

A human being is a deciding being. Viktor E. Frankl

Even a genius cannot completely resist his Zeitgeist, the spirit of his time. Viktor E. Frankl

Insight Question: What am I doing about the things that matter most in my life?

Religion is the search for ultimate meaning. Viktor E. Frankl

Logotherapy sees the human patient in all his humanness. I step up to the core of the patient's being. And that is a being in search of meaning, a being that is transcending himself, a being capable of acting in love for others. Viktor E. Frankl

The more one forgets himself - by giving himself to a cause to serve or another person to love - the more human he is. Viktor E. Frankl

We who lived in concentration camps can remember the men who walked through the huts comforting others, giving away their last piece of bread. Viktor E. Frankl

Ultimately, man should not ask what the meaning of his life is, but rather he must recognize that it is he who is asked. Viktor E. Frankl

Insight Question: At what time in my recent past have I felt most passionate and alive?

If you call 'religious' a man who believes in what I call a Supermeaning, a meaning so comprehensive that you can no longer grasp it, get hold of it in rational intellectual terminology, then one should feel free to call me religious, really. Viktor E. Frankl

To the European, it is a characteristic of the American culture that, again and again, one is commanded and ordered to 'be happy.' But happiness cannot be pursued; it must ensue. One must have a reason to 'be happy.' Viktor E. Frankl

Each man is questioned by life; and he can only answer to life by answering for his own life; to life he can only respond by being responsible. Viktor E. Frankl

No one can become fully aware of the very essence of another human being unless he loves him. Viktor E. Frankl

Faith is trust in ultimate meaning. Viktor E. Frankl

Fear may come true that which one is afraid of. Viktor E. Frankl

A painter tries to convey to us a picture of the world as he sees it; an ophthalmologist tries to enable us to see the world as it really is. The logotherapist's role consists of widening and broadening the visual field of the patient so that the whole spectrum of potential meaning becomes conscious and visible to him. Viktor E. Frankl

Insight Question: What is the difference between being alive and truly living?

Insight Question: What would I do differently if I knew nobody would judge me?

Letter to my past self (forgive self and others; move on)

Letter to my current self (convictions you've made; ambitions & goals; encouragement)

Letter to my future self (vision)

Write a letter to another person who is significant in your journey. How can you help him / her? What can he / she do to help you? This journey is a 'we,' and you will impact others just as you are impacted by them. Tell them about it here.

Write a letter to a second person who is significant in your journey. How can you help him / her? What can he / she do to help you? This journey is a 'we,' and you will impact others just as you are impacted by them. Tell them about it here

Genogram page. Draw a visual diagram of your family and friend relationships. Use the following key to guide you in your own family diagram. You can put family and friendships.

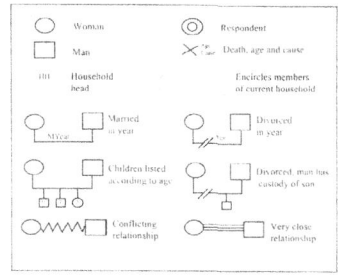

Thoughts

Thoughts

Thoughts

Thoughts

Thoughts

Therapeutic Journal Project:

001   It is the Forgotten Past that Enslaves Us (C.S. Lewis Quotes)

002   The Search for Meaning (Albert Camus & Viktor Frankl Quotes)

003   Keep Stillness Inside of You (Quotes on Peace)

004   The Best of All Things is to Learn (Quote by Louis L'Amour)

005   Existential Philosophers (Socrates, Plato, Kierkegaard)

006   I Was Born to be Awesome, Not Perfect (Quotes for Teens)

007   Quit or be Exceptional. Average is for Losers. (Quotes by Seth Godin)

008   Enjoy Your Ice Cream While It's On Your Plate (Quotes on Happiness)

009   Love Leaves a Memory No One Can Steal (Quotes on Healing)

010   There is No Worse Lie than a Truth Misunderstood (Quotes by William James)

011   I Am Strong Because I've Been Weak (Quotes on Excitement & Life)

012   Better a Cruel Truth than a Comfortable Delusion (Quotes from Edward Abbey)

Forthcoming:

Death & Dying   Proverbs

For Those Approaching Old Age

Carl Jung & Abraham Maslow

Alfred Ellis & Virginia Satir

Quotes from the *Tao Te Chung*

By David Dye, also available on Amazon

Together Alone

Desert Philosophizing: Ruminations Along the Burr Trail

Get up. Move. Do life.

Do life with passion!

This is your time!

Live Your Story!

Available on Amazon

Printed in Great Britain
by Amazon

29966289R00076